Crocheting Cats Items
Stunning Patterns to Craft for Your Loving Cats

DEDICATION

Contents

INTRODUCTION

Embark on a journey into the captivating world of crocheting, where creativity knows no bounds. Crochet, an art form that weaves together threads of imagination and craftsmanship, offers a gateway to express your creativity in ways both functional and artistic. With just a hook and some yarn, you can create intricate patterns, fashion beautiful accessories, and infuse your personal touch into every stitch.

In the realm of crochet, there's a vast array of possibilities, and in this book, we're about to explore a particularly endearing niche – Crocheting Items for Cats. As you delve into the pages that follow, you'll discover how this age-old craft can be transformed into a heartwarming way to pamper your feline friends. From cozy blankets that provide warmth on chilly nights to whimsical toys that will keep them entertained for hours and more cute items, you'll find a treasure trove of patterns and projects designed specifically for your beloved cats.

This book will give you everything you need for the project in the Prepping section. You're perfectly informed from the basis to the detail about the supplies and the stitches or abbreviations. Thence, it can be said that this paper is made for everyone whether you are familiar to crochet or not. And for the most interesting part, easy-to-follow patterns with pictures and instructions will definitely not disappoint you.

So, let your crochet journey begin, as we combine the artistry of crochet with the love we hold for our furry companions.

CHAPTER 1: FREQUENTLY ASKED QUESTIONS

Are Crochet Toys Safe For Cats?

Even though yarn balls are commonly depicted as a toy for cats, yarn can be really dangerous for our feline friends. Because of this, it's important to make sure any crochet toy yarn ends are secure and won't unravel. Yarn and other crochet projects should not be available to cats unless they're being supervised.

Are Crochet Collars Safe For Cats?

Collars that are crocheted should only be used when there is a human around to monitor the cat in case their claws get stuck in the fibers.

How Much Yarn Will You Need To Crochet A Cat Sweater?

Depending on the size of your cat or how many cat sweaters you are making, the size will vary. For small to medium sized cats, one skein of yarn will be more than enough. Don't worry; your pattern will let you know how much is necessary.

When Should Cats Wear Clothes/Sweaters?

Depending on the time of year, the climate where you live and how warm or cool you keep your house, hairless cats or cats with very short haircuts may appreciate the warmth provided by a cat sweater.

How To Pick The Right Crochet Sweater For Your Cat?

When choosing a sweater, consider what you would deem comfortable or uncomfortable. Avoid adding bells, bangles, or anything that can become detached easily that your cat might chew or choke on. To that end, you should always supervise your cat when he's wearing clothing, especially the first few times.

Is It Easy To Crochet A Cat Bed?

Crocheting allows you to make almost anything. From clothes to stuffed animals, if you can make the shape with yarn, then you can crochet it—and this includes cat beds. I recommend considering what type of bed your cat likes as well as your experience level when choosing a pattern. However, just because a bed looks more complicated doesn't make it harder. Many crochet patterns pull off premium-looking designs with minimum difficulty.

To wrap up: These crochet patterns for cats would be perfect gifts – because our four-legged members like presents too! Just because you catch your cats playing with cardboard or sleeping on a stray towel doesn't mean that they won't appreciate a regal stuffed sofa bed or a crocheted collar. So, why don't we move to the next step: preparing for the project!

CHAPTER 2: PREPPING

1. TOOLS AND MATERIALS

➤ **Yarn**

One of the many nice things about crochet is the wide variety of yarns you can work with. However, with so many choices, it can be overwhelming! So which yarn should you use, especially when you're new to crochet? A smooth yarn that feels good in your hands is the best choice when you're just starting. Choose a plain, soft yarn in a color you love, but avoid very dark colors at first. Your stitches will show more clearly with lighter-colored yarn. Novelty yarns with loops, bobbles, fluff, or glitter might be tempting right now, but they re more difficult to work with because the texture obscures your stitches. Wait until you have a thorough grasp of the basics of crochet before you attempt to work with one of these yarns.

Whatever yarn you choose, it will likely come wound in a skein, ball, or hank, most often with a paper ball band surrounding it. The ball band contains useful information about the yarn, including its weight, fiber composition, yardage, care instructions, and more.

You can crochet using the yarn tail found on the outside of the skein or fish out the tail from the middle of the skein (a center-pull skein). Some higher-end yarn is packaged in a hank—a large loop of yarn twisted into a coil. To avoid tangles when you crochet with a hank, undo the twisted coil and hand-wind the yarn into a ball or use a yarn winder to wind it into a center-pull skein.

Yarn Weights

The weight of a yarn refers to its thickness, not the weight of a ball or skein. Yarn varies in thickness from very thin lace weight (which you can crochet gossamer-fine shawls with) to super bulky (which is more suited for thick blankets and oversized chunky scarves) and every thickness in between. Lighter yarns need smaller hooks and take more stitches and rows to produce the same-sized piece of crocheted fabric you'd get with a heavier yarn paired with a larger hook.

When you're just beginning to learn to crochet, a medium-weight yarn is a good choice. Perfect for a wide range of projects, it's thick enough that you can easily see your stitches. Look for a worsted weight yarn. Depending on the manufacturer, it could also be called medium. #4, aran, or 10-ply.

Yarn Fibers

Yarn can be made from plant fibers (such as cotton, linen, and bamboo), animal fibers (such as wool, alpaca, mohair, and angora), and man-made fibers (such as acrylic, nylon, and microfiber).

- Cotton is strong, inelastic, and absorbent, which makes it a good choice for kitchen and bathroom items, such as dishcloths and washcloths. Mercerized cotton has been processed to make it strong, smooth, and shiny, but it's also less absorbent.
- Wool is light and stretchy and makes warm winter clothes. Check the care instructions carefully; most wool shrinks when washed.

Superwash wool has been treated so it can be machine washed without the fibers felting or binding together.

- Acrylic is inexpensive and easy to care for, but it can't tolerate heat. It's often available in a wide range of colors that make it particularly suitable for blankets and toys.

Yarn can also be produced from a blend of fibers, which combines the properties of each. For example, acrylic can be added to cotton to give it some stretch or added to wool to make it washable.

➢ Hook

Crochet hooks are available in a range of sizes, materials, and styles. A good hook feels comfortable in your hand and helps you form stitches without difficulty. With time and experimentation, you'll find the type of hook that works best for you and your crocheting style.

A crochet hook is made of a few basic parts: the point, throat, shaft, head, thumb rest, and handle:

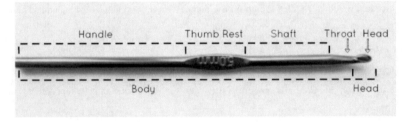

A pointier tip can get into tight stitches more easily, while a more rounded tip is less likely to split the yarn. The throat catches the yarn and the shank holds your working loops and determines your stitch size. The shape of the head varies by manufacturer. In-line hooks have the head directly in line with and the same size as the shaft, whereas tapered hooks have a more curved shape and a narrower throat.

The thumb grip helps you control and rotate the hook and the handle helps balance the hook while you crochet. If you have large hands, you might find a longer handle more comfortable. If holding a crochet hook is uncomfortable for you, try a hook with a cushioned or shaped handle.

Hook Sizes

The size of your hook, measured by the width across the shank, determines the size of the stitches you create. The hook size you need is related to the thickness of the yarn you choose: Thicker yarns require larger hooks.

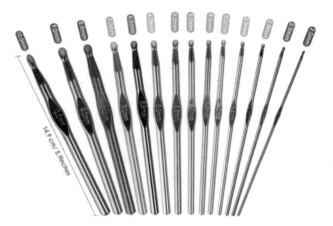

Crochet hooks are labeled in either U.S. or metric sizes or both. U.S. sizes are characterized by letters and/or numbers and the equivalent metric measurement is given in millimeters, as shown in the following table. Note that the U.S. letter/number size labels can vary among brands. If in doubt, check the metric size it's less ambiguous.

U.S. Size	Metric Size
B/1	2mm, 2.25mm
C/1	2.5mm, 2.75mm
D/3	3mm, 3.25mm
E/4	3.5mm
F/5	3.75mm, 4mm
G/6	4mm, 4.25mm
G/7	4.5mm
H/8	5mm
I/9	5.5mm
J/10	6mm
K/10.5	6.5mm, 7mm
L/11	8mm
M, N/13	9mm
N, P/15	10mm

For thread crochet, fine steel hooks are available in a range of very small sizes, numbered from U.S. 00 to 14 (decreasing from 3.5 to 0.75mm).

When you're starting out, it's best to use a medium hook size and a medium weight yarn) so the hook is easy to hold and maneuver and your stitches are large enough to see clearly. For your first hook, a U.S. H/8 (5mm) or U.S. 1/9 (5.5mm) is a good choice.

Hook Materials

- Ergonomic Hooks: If one has arthritis, carpal tunnel, or other health concerns, then the use of best ergonomic crochet hooks can alleviate the pain while crocheting. These hooks have large soft handles that allow inserting the hook you need to use for your project. It also comes with readymade handles and it makes you crochet for hours without feeling pain or cramping.

- Aluminum is smooth, strong, and long-lasting, but it might feel cold and inflexible in your hands.

- Plastic is smooth and inexpensive, but it makes a squeaky noise when used with some yarns and can bend or break relatively easily.

- Wood is lightweight and flexible, but it's prone to splintering or snapping, especially in smaller sizes.

- Steel is the strongest and come in the smallest sizes. If you want to crochet with thread, you'll likely use a very small stell crochet hook. They are durable and smooth, so working with them is easy, quick and pleasurable.

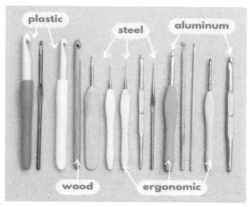

➢ **Other Tools You Need**

– **Yarn Needle** (also called a tapestry needle or darning needle) to weave in your yarn tails and stitch pieces together. Yarn needles are thick, blunt-tipped and have a large eye yo fit the yarn into.

– **Scissors**: are an essential tool for crochet. You'll use them to cut the yarn at the end of each piece and to trim yarn tails when you finish your work.

10

- **Measuring Tape** (or ruler): is invaluable for checking your gauge and the size of your finished pieces. .

- **Stitch Markers**: have multiple uses. You can use them to mark specific stitches in your crochet so you don't lose your place in a pattern, and more importantly, you can place a stitch marker in your working loop to save your work from unravelling when you put down your crochet.

- **Row Counter**: is usefull if you're likely to get distracted or you're working on a large piece. Just remember to advance the counter at the end of each row and you'll never lose your place.

- **Pins**: are essential if you're going to block your crochet. T-pins are good choice. They're long, sturdy, and easy to handle. Be sure to choose rustproof pins so you don't end up with rust stains ruining your handiwork.

2.   GUIDE TO READ A PATTERN

Reading a pattern with instructions for nine sizes can take some getting used to. At first glance, the numbers may seem overwhelming. but remember that when you take into account the numbers that apply to your size, the instructions are actually quite basic. You may want to circle the numbers that pertain to your size before beginning. Or, if you don't want to write in this book, you can take a picture of the pattern and digitize it or print it out to write on.

Each of the patterns has nine sizes ranging from XS to 5X except for a few oversized designs that have merged two or three sizes together while maintaining the same size range. Sizes are written as follows:

XS (S, M, L, XL) (2X, 3X, 4X, 5X). When working the pattern, you will only follow the numbers that pertain to your size.

For example: Sc in the next 3 (4, 5, 6, 7) (8, 9, 10, 11) sts.

This set of instructions means size XS will single crochet in the next 3 stitches, size L will single crochet in the next 6 stitches and size 5X will single crochet in the next 11 stitches. Two sets of parentheses are included to make it easier to find your size because it can look a bit jumbled when eight different numbers are written inside one set of parentheses. The number before the parentheses is the value for size XS, the first set of parentheses contain sizes S through XL, and the second set of parentheses contains sizes 2X through SX. Once you know the placement of your size, it will become second nature to follow the numbers written just for you. If only one value is provided, it applies to all sizes.

For example: Hdc in each st around for the next 4 rows.

This means that all sizes are instructed to half double crochet each stitch around for the next 4 rows.

Sometimes you are instructed to work until a specified measurement, rather than work a specified number of rows. Imperial and metric will always be provided, with imperial written first, followed by the corresponding metric units.

For example: Hdc in each st until work measures 12 inches (30 cm).

This means to work one half double crochet into each stitch until your work measures 12 inches (or 30 cm if you follow the metric units).

Symbols Used

[]Repeat the sequence inside the brackets as many times as indicated immediately following the brackets.

Example: [de in next st, sc in next st] 6 (6, 6, 6, 7) (7. 8, 8, 8) times.

() Work the sequence inside the parentheses into the same stitch/space.

Example: (sc, ch 2, dc) in next ch-sp.

*—Indicates the beginning of a sequence that is to be repeatad as many times as indicated.

Example 1: Ch 1, se in first sc, *ch 1, sk next ch-sp, sc in next sc; rep from * to end of row, turn.

Example 2: Ch 1, sc in next st, *dc in next st, sc in next st; rep from * 23 (26, 27, 31, 34) (37, 42, 44, 48) more times, turn.

* instructions within asterisks * Indicates to repeat the sequence in between the asterisks as many times as indicated.

Example: Ch 1, se in first sc, *ch 1, sk next ch-sp, sc in next sc*; rep from * to * across Side 1 until 1 ch-sp and 1 sc remain unworked.

3.   ABBREVIATIONS

- 2-dc CL: two double crochet cluster
- bo: bobble
- BPac: back post double crochet
- BPdc2tog: back post double crochet two together
- BPsc: back post single crochet
- CC: contrasting color:
- ch: chain stitch
- CL: cluster
- crossed CL: crossed cluster crossed de: crossed double crochet
- dc(s): double crochet
- de2tog: double crochet two stitches together
- FPdc: front post double crochet
- FPdc2tog: front post double crochet two together
- FPdc3tog: front post double crochet three together
- FPsc: front post single crochet
- FPtr: front post treble crochet
- FPtrtog: front post treble crochet three together
- Hdc: half double crochet
- MC: main color
- MR: magic ring
- rnd(s): round(s)

- RS: right side
- sc: single crochet
- sl st: slip stitch
- sp: space
- st(s): stitch(es)
- tr: treble crochet
- v-st: v stitch
- WS: wrong side
- yo: yarn over

Terminology

The patterns are written using US crochet terms. If you are used to working with UK terms, here's a guide to the relevant conversions for the stitch names:

US TERM	UK TERM
Single crochet	Double crochet
Half double crochet	Half treble crochet
Double crochet	Treble crochet
Treble crochet	Double treble crochet

4. BASIC STITCHES USED

➢ Chain Stitch

- Making a slip knot

- Yarn over the hook

Loop the working yarn over the hook from back to front. Either use your left hand to wrap the yarn over the crochet hook from behind and then over the top, or use your right hand to manipulate your hook to do the same thing.

- Draw through a loop

Pull the hook down and through the current loop on the hook. As you just finish drawing the yarn through, you will likely find it easier to complete the stitch if you return the hook to its original position facing upwards.

- Making a chain

You've just "chained one," making one chain stitch.

➤ **Slip Stitch**

  – Start the slip stitch

You can work a slip stitch at just about any point after you begin your project. If you already have an active loop on your crochet hook, insert your hook into the spot where you want to crochet the slip stitch. Then hook your yarn as pictured.

  – Pull yarn through

– Finish slip stitch

Finally, draw the newly created loop through the active loop on your hook. Once you try these steps a few times, it becomes almost like a single motion. The slip stitch is now complete.

➤ Single Crochet

– Insert crochet hook

After you form the foundation chain of stitches, insert the hook through the first chain. For the second row and beyond, insert your hook into the single crochet stitch directly below it in the row. Slide the hook under both loops on the top of the chain.

- Yarn over and grab the yarn

With the crochet hook in place, prepare to draw up a loop. Wrap the yarn over your crochet hook, and grab it with the hook.

- Draw up the loop

Pull or "draw" the hook and work yarn through the loops. You should now have two stitches or "loops" on your hook.

- Yarn over again

- Draw the yarn through both loops

Draw the hook and yarn through both of the loops on the hook. This completes the single crochet stitch. One loop remains on your crochet hook. This loop is the starting point for your next stitch. You can repeat this sequence of steps as many times as needed to create additional single crochet stitches across the row (or round).

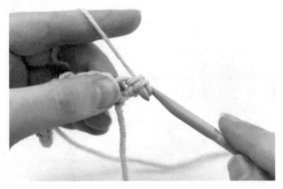

➤ Half Double Crochet Stitch

- Crochet a foundation chain

- Start in the correct chain

To work the first half double crochet into the foundation chain you will crochet into the chain that is three chains away from your hook.

When you crochet in rows, you begin the row with a turning chain. The height of the turning chain depends on the height of the crochet stitch. In half double crochet, chain two for a turning chain.

- Yarn over and insert the crochet hook

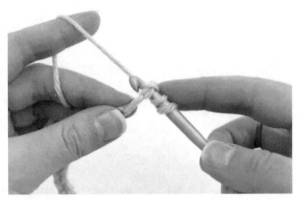

- Yarn over and pull through the stitch
- You should now have three loops on the hook.

    – Yarn over and pull through the loops

Yarn over one more time and pull the yarn through all three loops. That completes the first half double crochet stitch.

> **Double Crochet Stitch**

    – Begin with a foundation chain then yarn over

In most patterns you will start a row with a turning chain, which you see here under the hook. It usually counts as a stitch, and for double crochet consists of a chain 3; the three chain stitches are about the same height as a double crochet stitch. Your pattern will tell you whether or not to count it.

- Insert your crochet hook

- Draw through a loop, yarn over amd draw yarn through 2 loops

- Yarn over, draw through last 2 loops

➢ **Treble Crochet Stitch**

- Yarn over the hook twice (this means wrapping the yarn around the hook from back to front two times). Your hook should now have three loops on it.

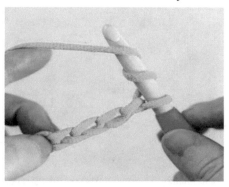

- Then, skip four chains and insert the hook into the fifth chain from the hook. (The four skipped chains count as the first stitch.)

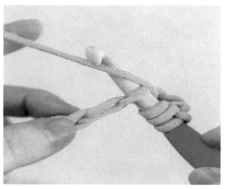

- Yarn over again and pull up a loop. You should have four loops on your hook.

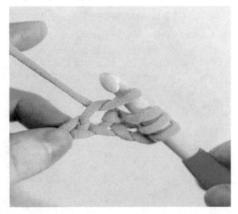

- Yarn over again and pull through two loops. You should now have three loops remaining on your hook.

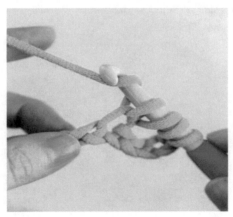

- Repeat the previous steps. You should now have two loops remaining on your hook.

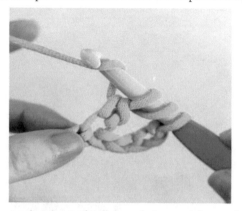

- Finally, yarn over one last time and pull through the remaining two loops. You've just made your first treble crochet stitch.

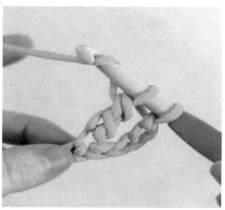

CHAPTER 3: PATTERNS

PART I: Playful Toys

1. **Stuffy and Puffy Balls**

Materials

- **Yarn**

  Lily® Sugar'n Cream® (Solids: 2.5 oz/70.9 g; 120 yds/109 m: Ombres: 2 oz/56.7 g; 95 yds/86 m)

  Main Color (MC) Batik Ombre (02446) or Robins Egg (01215) 1 ball

  Contrast A Hot Orange (01628) or Hot Green (01712) 1 ball

  Contrast B White (00001) 1 ball

- **Hook**

  Size U.S. F/5 (3.75 mm) crochet hook or size needed to obtain gauge.

- Stuffing

- Optional: Ball and bell cat toy to replace stuffing.

Measurements

Approx 3" [7.5 cm] in diameter, excluding fins.

Gauge

16 sc and 19 rows = 4" [10 cm].

Pattern

BODY

With A, ch 2.

Rnd 1: 8 sc in 2nd ch from hook. Join with sl st to first sc.

Rnd 2: Ch 1. Working in back loops only, (Sc2tog. 1 sc in each of next 2 sc) twice. Join MC with sl st to first sc. Break A. 6 sc.

Rnd 3: With MC, ch 1. Working in back loops only, 2 sc in each sc around. Join with sl st to first sc. 12 sc.

Rnd 4: Ch 1. *2 sc in next sc. Draw up a loop in next st. (Yoh and draw through 1 loop on hook) 3 times. Yoh and draw through 2 loops on hook – 1 sc picot (scp) made. Rep from * around. Join with sl st to first sc. 18 sts.

Rnd 5: Ch 1. *2 sc in next st. 1 sc in next st. 1 scp in next st. Rep from * around. Join with sl st to first sc. 24 sts.

Rnd 6 - 8: Ch 1. *1 sc in each of next 3 sts. 1 scp in next st. Rep from * around. Join with sl st to first st.

Rnd 9: Ch 1. *Sc2tog. 1 sc in next st. 1 scp in next st. Rep from * around. Join with sl st to first st. 18 sts.

Rnd 10: Ch 1. *Sc2tog. 1 scp in next st

Rep from * around. Join with sl st to first st. 12 sts. Stuff Body lightly.

Optional: Insert ball and bell toy.

Rnd 11: Ch 1. *Sc2tog. Rep from * around. Join with sl st to first st. 6 sts.

Fasten off.

TAIL

Folding last rnd of Body flat and working through both thicknesses, join A with sl st to first sc.

Row 1: Ch 1. 1 sc same sp as last sl st. 1 sc in each of next 2 sc. Turn.

Row 2: Ch 3 (counts as dc). 2 dc in first sc. 3 dc in each of next 2 sc.

Fasten off.

FINS (make 2)

With A, ch 4.

Row 1: 4 dc in 4th ch from hook.

Fasten off.

EYES (make 2)

With B, ch 2.

Rnd 1: 5 sc in 2nd ch from hook. Join with sl st to first sc.

Fasten off.

FINISHING

Sew Fins and Eyes to Body as seen in picture. With MC, embroider pupils in center of Eyes with French knots.

2. Ring-a-ling Crochet Bell

Materials

- Medium weight yarn
- Crochet hook (5.00mm H hook)
- Toilet paper tube (I used 1/2 a roll for the small cat toy and a full roll for the large toy)
- Bell
- Needle and thread
- Darning Needle to weave in ends
- Scissors

Pattern

Rnd 1: (Ch) 20, join with (sl st) to form ring (keeping tension firm but not tight – you want both ends to be a little tighter so they hug around the toilet paper tube).

Make sure to not to twist your stitches.

Rnd 2: (Ch) 2 in first chain and then (dc) in each remaining stitch in round. (Sl st) in last stitch in round to join.

Repeat for 7 rounds for 1/2 toilet paper roll size toy or 11 rounds for full toilet paper roll.

Rnd 3: Finish off last round with 1 (sl st) in each stitch and join.

Rnd 4: Ch 30 then make 2 (dc) in the 3rd chain from the hook. (If you'd like a longer curlicue than make the chain longer).

Rnd 5: Make 3 (dc) in each chain until you get back to the start of the chain. (Sl st) to join. Fasten off and weave in ends.

Rnd 6: Sew bell on end of curlicue.

Rnd 7: Fit over toilet paper roll.

And that's it, you now complete your work!

3. Swirly Toys

Materials

- **Yarn:** For 3 cat toys you will need approximately 1/2 oz, each of a variegated and a solid color medium weight (worsted) yarn.

  Colors used in the sample project: Red Heart variegated Mexicana (color #0950) Red Heart solid colors: Royal Blue (#0385), Bright Yellow (#0324), Cherry Red (#0319)

- **Hook**

  Size K (6.5 mm) hook

- Yarn needle

Gauge

5 sc = 2", but gauge is not important for overall pattern.

Finished size:

5 1/2" from tip of toy to knot, 10 1/2" long including yarn ends.

Note

- The entire cat toy is worked holding two strands of yarn together, one in a variegated and one in a solid color yarn.
- Leaving a 9 inch tail, ch 26 loosely.

Pattern

Rnd 1: Working into the back ridge of the starting chain, work 2 dc in the 4th ch from hook. Work 3 dc in each of the next 8 chs. Sc in the rem 14 chs. Fasten off, leaving a 9 inch yarn end.

Rnd 2: Using a yarn needle, thread these 2 ends through the beginning knot of the ch sts. (see photo A) Make a knot at this same spot securing all 4 ends.

Rnd 3: Trim yarn ends to 5 1/2 inches, and knot each yarn end individually at the bottom to prevent fraying.

The dc groups as well as the sc sts will naturally curl up giving the toy its swirly, curly fun. You can fluff it up a bit by separating the swirls before giving it your cat.

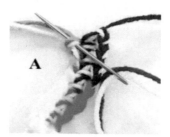

Helps and Hints

Working into the back ridge of starting chain: With the front of your starting chain facing you (photo B), roll your chain over so the back center loops are facing you (photo C). Work your stitches through these loops only. This will give your beginning edge the same look as your last row top stitches. It's especially helpful when you won't be adding a border, and I use this technique all the time when beginning row projects.

4. Triple Fishy Crochet Toy

Materials

- Yarn

  1 skein of Red Heart Yarn in your favourite color; Pictured in Light Lavender, Parakeet, and Yellow (or any worsted weight acrylic yarn)
- Hook

  Size 4.00 crochet hook
- Fiberfill
- Catnip
- Scissors
- Yarn needle

Note

Begin each round with a chain 1, and start the first stitch of the round in the same stitch as the chain 1. When ending the round, join using slip stitch with the 1st stitch of the round and NOT the chain 1.

Pattern

Rnd 1: 8 sc in magic ring

Rnd 2: *inc, sc; repeat from * to end (12)

Rnd 3: repeat round 2 (18)

Rnd 4: sc to end

Rnd 5 – 10: repeat round 4

Rnd 11: *sc, dec; repeat from * to end (12). Begin to fill with fiberfill and catnip.

Rnd 12: sc to end

Rnd 13: repeat round 11 (8)

Rnd 14: inc in each stitch (16)

Rnd 15 – 17: sc to end. Fill the tail with fiberfill and catnip. Do not overstuff.

Lay fish flat on its side, and use your hands to shape the fish so that it lays flat on it's side without being twisted.

Line up the edges of the open tail, chain 1 and sc the two tail edges together to seam the tail closed.

Cut yarn and weave in any ends.

Eyes placement:

- With a scrap piece of yarn in a contrasting color, thread your yarn needle and insert into fish where you would like the eye to be placed.
- Push needle through and out the other side of the fish.
- Insert needle back into the fish in a stitch next to the one you just came out of and back through to the side where you began.
- Tie the two yarn ends with a knot, and cut short.

Whip up a few more in your favorite colors, and your kitty will love you forever!

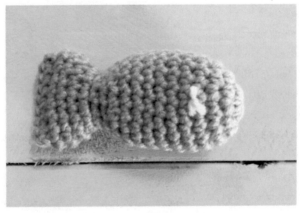

5. Harry The Toy Blanket

Materials

- Yarn

  Yarn of your choice, the pattern used an apparently 8 ply yarn from an Australian Dollarstore.

- Hook

  Hook size which matches your yarn, the pattern used a 7 mm hook.

- 2 or more jingle bells

- Tapestry needle

- Scissors

Pattern

If you want to end up with a bigger blanket just add multiples of 3 ch's st to your starting ch.

ch 31

Row 1: dc (*tr*) in 4 ch from hook, ch 1, dc (*tr*) in next st, *skip next ch, dc (*tr*), ch 1, dc (*tr*)* 7 times, dc (*tr*) in last ch

Row 2-13: ch 3, *dc (*tr*), ch 1, dc (*tr*)* 7 times, dc (*tr*) in last st.

hdc (*htr*) around your blanket to give it a smooth finish.

Make 15 fsc (*fdc*) at the place of your choice and attach a jingle bell to it.

Add as many tassels as you fancy.

Complete and then give it to your cat to enjoy!

PART 2: Accessories and Clothes

1. Yellow Bucket Hat

Materials

- Yarn (Yellow Color) Light or Medium Weight
- Corresponding Crochet Hook
- Scissors
- Tapesry Needle

Pattern

TOP OF HAT

Rnd 1: Make a magic loop, C 2, DC 10 into the magic loop. Sinch the tail to make the circle tight. SS into the first DC. (11)

Rnd 2: C 2, DC INC in every stitch (2 DC in every stitch). SS into first DC. (21)

Rnd 3: C 2, INC in every 2nd Stitch (Starting with 1DC, alternate 1 DC and 2 DC all the way around), SS into 1st DC. (31)

SIDE OF HAT

Rnd 4: C 2, in back loops only DC in every stitch around. SS into 1st DC. (31)

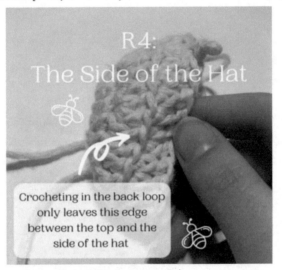

Rnd 5-6: C2, DC into each stitch all the way around. (31)

Rnd 7 (Ear Holes): C 2, DC into next 5 stitches, C 12, skip next 6 stitches, DC into 7th stitch. DC into next 7 stitches, C 12, Skip the next 6 stitches, DC into 7th stitch. DC into the next 5 stitches. SS into 1st DC. (46)

Rnd 8 (Straps): C 1, SC into 1st stitch, SC into next 11 stitches, C 41, SS into each C. SC into next 20 stitches, C 41, SS into each C, SC into next 12 stitches. SS into first SC. (46)

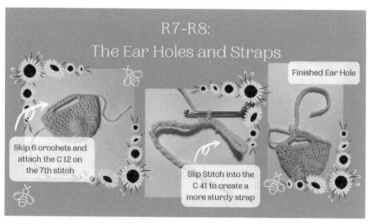

R7-R8:
The Ear Holes and Straps

Finished Ear Hole

Skip 6 crochets and attach the C 12 on the 7th stitch

Slip Stitch into the C 41 to create a more sturdy strap

BRIM OF HAT

Rnd 9: C 2, in front loops only, INC every 4th stitch (DC 1 into 3 stitches then DC 2 into the next). (48)

Rnd 10: DC into each stitch around. SS into first DC (48)

Tie off and you are finished!

2. Little Dark Witchy Hat

Materials

- Two Different Colors of Yarn (Any Color) Light or Medium Weight
- Corresponding Crochet Hook
- Scissors
- Tapestry needle
- Stitch Markers

Pattern

THE TOP OF THE HAT

Create a Magic Circle

Rnd 1: Chain1, DC 4 into magic ring (4)

Rnd 2: SS into the first DC, Chain 1, DC into the same stitch as Chain, (DC, DC INC) 2, DC (7)

Rnd 3: SS into the first DC, Chain 1, DC into the same stitch as Chain, (2 DC, DC INC) 2, DC (9)

Rnd 4: SS into the first DC, Chain 1, DC into the same stitch as Chain (3 DC, DC INC) 2, DC (11)

Rnd 5: SS into the first DC, Chain 1, DC into the same stitch as Chain (3 DC, DC INC) 2, 3 DC (13)

Rnd 6: Sl st into the first DC, Chain 1, DC into the same stitch as Chain (2 DC, DC INC) 4 (15)

Rnd 7: Dc in each stitch around (15)

Sl st into the first DC, Pull yarn through and cut leaving a tail.

MAKE THE BAND

Switch to the second color yarn.

Rnd 8: (3 SC, SC INC) 4 (20)

Rnd 9: Sl st into the first SC, Chain 1, SC into the same stitch as Chain, (4 SC, SC INC) 4, SC (23)

Sl st into the first SC, Pull yarn through, and cut leaving a tail.

Switch back to the first color yarn.

Rnd 10: Sl st into the first DC, (3 DC, DC INC) 6, DC (30)

Switch to the Second Color

EAR HOLES

Rnd 11: Sl st into the first DC, 4 DC, Chain 12, skip 6 stitches, and DC into 7th from Chain, 7 DC, Chain 12, skip 6 stitches, and DC into 7th from the Chain (43)

Adjust the amount of chains to make the ear holes bigger/ smaller

Rnd 12: Sl st into the first DC, (3 DC, DC INC) 8 (52)

Rnd 13: Sl st into the first DC, (4 DC, DC INC) 8 (58)

ADD THE TIES

Chain 50, starting on the second chain from the hook, slip stitch back in all the loops (Make 2)

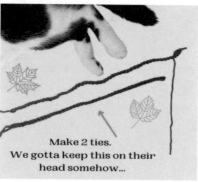

**Make 2 ties.
We gotta keep this on their head somehow...**

End off each tie and leave the yarn kinda long.

Attach the ties to the hat with a knot, then weave in the ends. Center each tie in the middle of the ear holes.

Wave in all ends and that's all there is.

See the picture below.

3. Hennin Crochet Hat

Materials

- Yarn: Yarn Bee Soft & Sleek DK (#3 weight)

    Color A: Pumpkin Paradise

    Color B: Oxblood

    Color C: Dijon

- Size 7/4.5mm crochet hook
- Stitch markers
- Tapestry needle

Finished Measurement

Neck opening circumference: 8 inches

Notes

- This hat is worked in rounds.
- Beginning ch 1 or ch 2 does not count as a stitch.
- First stitch of each round is worked in the same stitch as beginning chain.
- At the end of each round, sl st in the first stitch from previous round to join.
- The instructions in this pattern are for an adult size hairless cat.
- The sizing provided in this pattern is approximate. Depending on your tension and yarn choices, the finished measurement may vary. You may try using a larger or smaller size hook to obtain your desired measurement.

Pattern

EAR COVER - make two with color A and color B

FSC 40. (40)

Rnd 1: Ch 1. Sc in same st and across. (40)

Rnd 2: Ch 1. Sc2tog, sc in next 36 sts, sc2tog. (38)

Rnd 3: Ch 1. Sc2tog, sc in next 34 sts, sc2tog. (36)

Rnd 4: Ch 1. Sc2tog, sc in next 32 sts, sc2tog. (34)

Rnd 5: Ch 1. *Sc2tog, sc in next 14 sts* 2 times, sc2tog. (31)

Rnd 6: Ch 1. Sc2tog, sc in next 27 sts, sc2tog. (29)

Rnd 7: Ch 1. Sc2tog, sc in next 25 sts, sc2tog. (27)

Rnd 8: Ch 1. Sc2tog, sc in next 23 sts, sc2tog. (25)

Rnd 9: Ch 1. Sc2tog, sc in next 21 sts, sc2tog. (23)

Rnd 10: Ch 1. Sc2tog, sc in next 19 sts, sc2tog. (21)

Rnd 11: Ch 1. Sc2tog, sc in next 17 sts, sc2tog. (19)

Rnd 12: Ch 1. Sc2tog, sc in next 15 sts, sc2tog. (17)

Rnd 13: Ch 1. Sc2tog, sc in each st across. (16)

Rnd 14: Ch 1. Sc2tog, sc in next 12 sts, sc2tog. (14)

Rnd 15: Ch 1. Sc2tog, sc in each st across. (13)

Rnd 16: Ch 1. Sc2tog, sc in next 9 sts, sc2tog. (11)

Rnd 17: Ch 1. Sc2tog, sc in each st across. (10)

Rnd 18: Ch 1. Sc2tog, sc in next 6 sts, sc2tog. (8)

Rnd 19: Ch 1. Sc2tog, sc in each st across. (7)

Rnd 20: Ch 1. Sc2tog, sc in next 3 sts, sc2tog. (5)

Rnd 21: Ch 1. Sc2tog, sc in next 1 sts, sc2tog. (3) Sl st in the first stitch from previous round to join.

Cut yarn and tie off.

Repeat above steps for the second ear cover.

Sew Ear Covers Together

Find the two center sts on short side of each piece, place stitch marks in these sts. (Figure 1)

Place a stitch marker in the 5th st from the center sts on each side. (Figure 2)

With the right sides facing together, join these 12 sts with sl sts. (Figure 3)

Cut yarn and tie off.

BACK AND NECK

Switch to color C. Place the ear covers upside-down.

Attach yarn to first st from the middle of ear cover on your left. (Figure 4)

Tip: this is the st next to the last st joined from step above in **Sew Ear Covers Together**.

Rnd 1: Ch 1. Sc in same st and next 13 sts, 2 sc in the space between the last st and next st (Figure 5), sc in next 28 sts, 2 sc in the space between the last st and next st, sc in next 14 sts. (60)

Rnd 2: Ch 1. Hdc2tog, hdc blo in next 12 sts, hdc2tog blo, hdc blo in next 13 sts, hdc2tog blo, hdc blo in next 13 sts, hdc2tog blo, hdc blo in next 14 sts. (56)

Rnd 3 (face opening round): Ch 2. Dc2tog, dc in next 5 sts, hdc in next 5 sts, sc in next 3 sts, ch 12. Skip 26 sts, sc in next 3 sts, hdc in next 5 sts, dc in next 5 sts, dc2tog. (40: 28 sts, 12 chs)

Rnd 4: Ch 2. Dc in same st and next 12 sts, hdc in next st, hdc in each of the 12 chs, hdc in next st, dc in next 13 sts. (40)

Rnd 5: Ch 2. Fpdc in same st, *bpdc in next st, fpdc in next st* 6 times, *bphdc in next st, fphdc in next st* 7 times, *bpdc in next st, fpdc in next st* 6 times, bpdc in last st. (40)

Rnd 6-9: Repeat Round 5.

Cut yarn and tie off.

FINISHING UP

Face opening

Attach yarn in any st. Ch 1, sc in same st and around evenly. (40)

Sew in all ends.

4. Small Viking Crochet Hat

Materials

- Yarn

  Worsted weight yarn in 2 colors, the pattern used Hawk and Whisker

  18 yards for the smaller and 21 yards for the larger hat

- Hook

  Size 4.5mm

- Small amount of polyester stuffing for the horns

- Scissors

- Stitch markers

Pattern

ch 2

Rnd 1. 6 sc in 2nd ch from hook. (6)

Rnd 2. 2 sc in each st (12)

Rnd 3. (2sc in next st, sc in next st) repeat around (18)

Rnd 4. Sc around

Rnd 5. (2sc in the next st, sc in the next 2 sts) repeat around (24)

Rnd 6. Sc around

Rnd 7. (2 sc in next st, sc in next 3 sts) repeat around (30)

Rnd 8. Sc around

Rnd 9. (2 sc in next st, sc in next 4 sts) repeat around (36) these next 2 rows are for the larger size

Rnd 10. Sc around

Rnd 11. (Sc 2 in next st, sc in next 5 sts) (42)

FOR SMALLER SIZE

At end of round 9, ch 12, skip 7 sts, sc next 11 sts, ch 12, skip 7 sts, sc in next 10 sts, sl st to beginning sc. Weave in ends and close up hole at top.

FOR LARGER SIZE

At end of round 11, ch 14, skip 8 sts, sc next 13 sts, ch 14, sk 8 sts, sc in next 12 sts, sl st to beginning sc. Weave in ends and close up hole at top.

HORNS (make 2 for both sizes)

Leaving a long tail for sewing, ch 12, join to form ring

Rnd 1. Sc in each ch around (12)

Rnd 2. Sc in next 4 sts, hdc in next 5 sts, sc 3 (12)

Rnd 3. Sc2tog, sc in next 2 sts, hdc in next 5 sts, sc in next st, sc2tog (10)

Rnd 4. Sc2tog, sc in next st, hdc in next 5 sts, sc2tog (8)

Rnd 5. Sc2tog around (4)

Rnd 6. Draw end through 4 sts and weave in end.

Lightly stuff each horn and stitch above ear loops on hat with points facing upward.

5. Fur – Trimmed Sweater

Materials

- Yarn:

Main Color :skeins (255 yd ea) Bernat® Soft Bouclé or 5/bulky weight yarn

Contrasting Color – 1 skein (71 yd) Bernat® Boa or 5/bulky weight eyelash

- Hook

Size J-10 (6.0 mm) crochet hook or size to obtain gauge

Size K-10.5 (6.5 mm) crochet hook or size to obtain gauge

- Stitch markers
- Yarn needle

Gauge

15 sc and 20 rows = 5"

Finished Size

Size Chart

	XS	S	M	L	XL	XXL	XXXL
Length	5-8"	8-11"	11-14"	14-17"	17-20"	20-23"	23-26"
Chest	Up to 10"	10-15"	15-20"	20-25"	25-30"	30-35"	35-40"
Neck	Up to 7"	7-10"	10-13"	13-16"	16-19"	19-22"	21-25"

*Length = collar to base of tail. Chest = girth of chest at widest point.

Pattern

Worked from neck to chest

With MC and K hook, ch 25 (35, 43, 53, 61, 67, 77).

Row 1 (RS). Sc in 2nd ch from hook and in each across. 24 (34, 42, 52, 60, 66, 76) sc.

Row 2 (WS). Ch 1; turn. 2 sc in 1st sc, 1 sc in ea of next sc across to last sc, 2 sc in last sc. 26 (36, 44, 54, 62, 68, 78) sc.

Rows 3-6 (3-8, 3-12, 3-14, 3-18, 3-22, 3-25). Rep row 2. 34 (48, 64, 78, 94, 108, 124) sc.

Row 7 (9, 13, 15, 19, 23, 26). Ch 1; turn. Sc in next 4 (6, 8, 10, 12, 14, 16) sc; place stitch marker for right leg shaping. Sc in next 23 (31, 41, 49, 59, 69, 81) sc; place stitch marker for center section. Sc in ea rem sc across.

LEFT LEG SHAPING

Row 8 (10, 14, 16, 20, 24, 27). Ch 1; turn. Sc in next 4 (6, 8, 10, 12, 14, 16) sc; leave rem sc un-worked. 4 (6, 8, 10, 12, 14, 16) sc.

Rows 9-10 (11-14, 15-20, 17-24, 21-30, 25-34, 28-37). Ch 1; turn.

Sc in ea sc across.

Finish off.

CENTER SECTION

With WS facing, join MC with sl st to row 7 (9, 13, 15, 19, 23, 26) in sc where marker was placed for center shaping. There will be 3(5, 7, 9, 11, 11, 11) sc left un-worked between left leg shaping and center section.

Row 8 (10, 14, 16, 20, 24, 27). Sc in same so as joining and next 19 (25, 29, 39, 47,57, 69) sc; leave rem so un-worked. 20 (26, 30, 40, 48, 58, 70) sc.

Rows 9-10 (11-14, 15-20, 17-24, 21-30, 25-34, 28-37). Ch 1; turn. Sc in ea sc across.

Finish off.

RIGHT LEG SHAPING

With WS facing, join MC with sl st to row 7 (9, 13, 15, 19, 23, 26) in sc where marker was placed for right leg shaping. There will be 3 (5, 7, 9, 11, 11, 11) sc left un-worked between center section and right leg shaping.

Row 8 (10, 14, 16, 20, 24, 27). Sc in same so as joining and ea sc across. 4 (6, 8, 10, 12, 14, 16) sc.

Rows 9-10 (11-14, 15-20, 17-24, 21-30, 25-34, 28-37). Ch 1; turn. Sc in ea sc across. Do not finish off.

BODY

Row 11 (15, 21, 25, 31, 35, 38). Ch 1; turn. Sc in next 4 (6, 8, 10, 12, 14, 16) sc, ch 3 (5, 7, 9, 11, 11, 11), sc in ea sc across intes actios et leg shaping. 2(38) 50, 60, 72, 86, 102) sc and 2 ch sp.

Row 12 (16, 22, 26, 32, 36, 39). Ch 1; turn. Sc in next 4 (6, 8, 10, 12, 14, 16) sc, 3 (5, 7, 9, 11, 11, 11) sc in next ch sp, sc in next 20 (26, 30, 40, 48, 58, 70) sc, 3 (5, 7, 9, 11, 11, 11) sc in next ch sp, sc in ca sc across. 34 (48, 64, 78, 94, 108, 124) sc.

Rows 13-20 (17-28, 23-36, 27-44, 33-52, 37-60, 40-68). Ch 1; turn. So in ea sc across.

Row 21 (29, 37, 45, 53, 61, 69). Ch 1; turn. Sc in 1st sc; place stitch marker for neck seam. Sc in ea of next so across; place 2nd marker for neck seam.

Row 22 (30, 38, 46, 54, 62, 70). Turn. Sl st in next 4 (6, 8, 10, 12, 14, 16) so, sc in next 26 (36, 48, 58, 70, 80, 92) sc, sl st in next sc; leave rem so un-worked. 26 (36, 48, 58, 70, 80, 92) sc.

Row 23 (31, 39, 47, 55, 63, 71). Ch 1; turn. Dec 1 sc in next 2 sc, sc in ea of next so across to last 2 sc; dec 1 sc in last 2 sc. 24 (34, 46, 56, 68, 78, 90) st.

Row 24 (32, 40, 48, 56, 64, 72). Ch 1; turn. Sc in ea st across.

Rows 25-26 (33-38, 41-50, 49-62, 57-74, 65-82, 73-90). Rep rows 23 & 24 (31 & 32, 39 & 40, 47 & 48, 55 & 56, 63 & 64, 71 & 72). 20 (28, 36, 42, 50, 60, 72) sc.

Row 27 (39, 51, 63, 75, 83, 91). Rep row 23 (31, 39, 47, 55, 63, 71). 18 (26, 34, 40, 48, 58, 70) sc.

Rows 28-32 (40-44, 52-56, 64-68, 76-80, 84-92, 92-104). Rep row 24 (32, 40, 48, 56, 64, 72). Finish off.

FINISHING

With WS facing, whipstitch neck seam from stitch markers placed to collar. Turn right side out.

EDGING

Neck and leg holes:

With RS facing and I hook, join CC to any so in neck edge.

Rnd 1. Ch 2; do not turn. Skip same sc as joining; de in ea of next sc around. Beg ch counts as do this row only.

Rnd 2. Ch 2; do not turn. Fpdc around 1st st, bpdc around next st, *fpdc around next st, bpdc around next st; rep from * around.

Rnd 3 (3, 3-4, 3-4, 3-5, 3-5, 3-5). Rep md 2.

Finish off. Rep for ea of the leg holes.

BELLY

With RS facing and I hook, join contrasting color to any sc in body edge. Ch 1; do not turn. So around body edge, working 1 sc in ea st and ea end of rows. Finish off. Weave in all ends.

6. Josephine Kitty Sweater

Materials

- Using a size K (6.50 MM) hook
- Red Heart Super Saver Yarn
- Scissors
- Stitch Markers

Pattern

Begin by shaping the chest and creating the sleeve holes:

Rnd 1: Ch 42 loosely, Jn with sl st in first ch to form a large ring. Ch 2, (counts as first dc here and throughout), 2 dc in same ch, sk next 2 ch, (3 dc in next ch, sk next 2 ch) around. Jn with sl st in first dc.

Fasten off if changing colors at the end of each row. If not simply sl st to the nearest place that you are instructed to begin. (14 sets of 3-dc-fans.)

Rnd 2: Jn with a sl st between any two fan clusters. Ch 2, 2 dc in same space. To form first arm hole, *put only 2 dc in next space between fans, chain 5 loosely, sk next space between fans and put 2 dc in the next space between fans.* 3 dc in next space. To make second armhole, repeat from * to *.

Then put 3 dc in each space the rest of the way around and jn with a sl st in the first dc. (8 sets of 3-dc-fans, 4 sets of 2-dc fans, and two armholes.)

Rnd 3: Jn with a sl st between one of the clusters. Ch 2, 2 dc in same space. 3 dc in each space around except in the two armholes. Work 5 dc in each armhole. Join with a sl st in first dc.

Rnd 4: Jn with a sl st between the cluster right before the first armhole. 2 dc in same space, sk next 2 st, 3 dc in next st (about the center of the 5 double crochets along the armhole), 3 dc in each of next 3 spaces between the fans, sk next 2 st, 3 dc in next st (also about the center of the

72

5 double crochets of this second armhole), 3 dc in each of the spaces between the fans around. Jn with a sl st in first dc. (14 3-dc-fan-clusters in all.)

Rnds 5 and 6: Jn with a sl st between one of the clusters. Ch 2, dc in same st, 3 dc in each space between the fan clusters around. Jn with a sl st in first dc.

Now will begin working back and forth in rows instead of around.

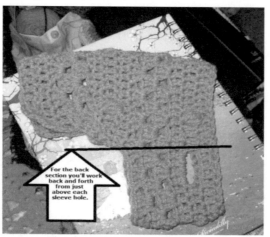

Row 1: Jn with a sl st in a space between fans that is even with the outside (upper) point of the closest armhole so that your rows will be starting just above one armhole and ending just above the other armhole back and forth. Ch 1, (sc, hdc, dc) in same space as join. Work 3 dc until you reach the space even with just above the other armhole. (dc, hdc, sc, ch 1, sl st) in that last space.

Row 2: Jn with a sl st in the last sc of previous row. Ch 1, turn. sc in next st (not the same st as your ch-1, but the hdc from the previous row), hdc in the next st, ch 1, 3 dc in the second space between fan stitches rather than the space that is now directly below your hdc. 3 dc in each space across stopping before last space.Ch 1, hdc in 3rd st from end, sc in 2nd st from end, sl st in the last st of the row. Fasten off.

Row 3: You don't have to turn rows anymore unless you're using the same color and working back and forth. If you're changing colors you might as well keep working with the right side facing you on every row now. Jn with a sl st in 1st st. (This should be between the sc/sl st spot of previous row.) Ch 1, (sc, hdc, dc) in same st, 3 dc in every space between fans across. After the last fan, sk the next st and in the very last st of the row (this should be between the sc/sl st of previous row) work (dc, hdc, sc, ch 1, sl st) in that last st.

Row 4 -7: Repeat Row 2 and 3 twice.

Row 8: Repeat Row 2.

FRONT SECTION: (Basically this will fill in the bottom half of the front of the sweater.) Working with the original chain you made to begin the sweater, you'll join with a sl st along the bottom section of the front just in line with the outside of one of the legs like you did on the other side of the sweater to create the back and forth rows of the sweater's back. Then you'll work across until you reach even with the outside of the opposite leg hole. You'll be turning and working back and forth, and as you move up the rows it will make a kind of square which you'll then fold up toward the neck/chest and sew it in place leaving only the opening for the neck.

Row 1: Jn with a sl st in the original chain just in line with the outside of one of the leg holes. You'll be joining in one of the spaces between the fans, only from the angel of the chain along the bottom and working in the opposite direction. Ch 2, dc only once in the same space, 3 dc in each space between the fans until you reach the fan space that is even with the outside of the second leg hole. Work only 2 dc in that last space.

74

Front flap will fold up toward the neck direction, but you will leave a neck hole as sewing in place.

Row 2: Jn with a sl st in the first st of the row. Ch 2, 3 dc in each space between the fans across. Work one dc in very last st.

Row 3: Jn with a sl st in first st. Ch 2, dc only once in the same space, 3 dc in each space between the fan across. Then work 2 dc in the very last space. Fasten off after row 3.

Fold the square section to fit along the bottom section of the front of the sweater. Use a yarn needle and pick a suitable color yarn to sew this flap section into place along the chain at the sides leaving only the neck hole at the top where you'll then be able to work around to form a colar or turtleneck.

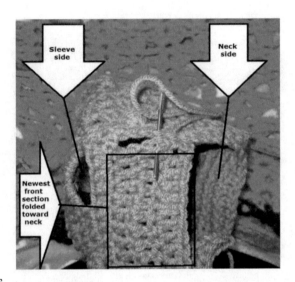

SLEEVES

Rnd 1: Around each armhole, there should be about 5 spaces that are like the spaces between the 3-dc-fans. Jn with a sl st in one of these spaces, ch 2, 2 dc in same space as join, then you'll put 3 dc in each space around accept for the little span of 5 dc in a row where you need to pick a spot about mid-way bewteen those stitches and add one more set of 3 dc in one st. This should give you 6 even 3-dc-fans to form the shape of the sleeve, and you'll join with a sl st in top of the first dc/ch-2.

Then make the sleeves as long as you'd like by joining next rnd with a sl st in any space between the fans, ch 2, dc in same space, then 3 dc in each space around and jn with a sl st in top of first dc/ch-2. I usually just add 2 rows, but you might be in the mood some time for some long pet sleeves! Fasten off at the end of your last row and weave in ends.

76

NECK

Rnd 1 and 2: Jn with sl st in any of the open spaces along the neck. Ch 2, 2dc in same space, 3 dc in next space and in each space around. Jn with a sl st in top of first dc.

Border:

For the border, jn with the color of your choice with a sl st somewhere along the edging. (Ch 1, sl st) around. Jn with sl st, fasten off, weave in ends.

7. Colorful Crochet Sweater

Materials

- Yarn

  Mary Maxim Sunrise (CDN) Shown in Desert Rose & Fossil, Light Weight #3, 240yds/100g, 100% premium micro acrylic

  Mary Maxim Lullaby (CDN) Shown in Cuddles, Light Weight #3, 236yds/100g, 100%premium micro acrylic

  XS (S, M, L) 1 ball each size, 65 (95, 160, 200) yards

- Hook

  US G/6 (4mm)

- Yarn Needle

- Scissors

- Measuring Tape

Sizing

The XS size is designed to fit a kitten approximately 5-8 weeks. S, 8-12 weeks. M, small-medium adult cat. L, large adult cat.

To size your pet as you go. Crochet the collar in multiples of 8 rows. Test on your pet for the correct size making sure it's not too tight. Follow the yoke pattern altering each section in increments of 2 sts if required. Continue increasing the yoke to fit your pet. Continue working the body as long as needed. Try on your pet as you go and make any necessary adjustments.

SIZE	XS	S	M	L
Finished Chest (IN)	8.5	10.5	13.5	15.5
Balls	1	1	1	1
Yards	65	95	160	200

Notes

The pullover is worked from the top down in the round. The collar is completed first by working in rows. It is then slip-stitched together, and the pullover begins by working around the collar's edge. Work the pullover in rounds until the required size is reached. The pattern is written for the smallest size, with the larger sizes in parentheses ( ). If there is only 1 number, it applies to all sizes—a step-by-step video tutorial is provided on YouTube for the XS size

Pattern

COLLAR

Row 1 (WS):

With the smaller hook, ch 5 (6, 6, 7) 1 sc in the 2nd ch from hook, 1 sc in each ch across, turn—4 (5, 5, 6) sts.

Row 2 (RS):

Ch 1 (not included as a st here and throughout), 1 sc in the blo of each st across, turn—4 (5, 5, 6) sts.

Rows 3- 32 (40, 48, 48):

Rep Row 2. After the final Row, ch 1, fold collar RS facing and sl st together (work through the blo). Flip the collar so that the seam is to the inside.

YOKE

Setup Round:

Ch 1, work sc sts evenly around the collar (1 st/row), sl st in the first sc to join—32 (40, 48, 48) sts.

Rnd 1: Ch 3 (counts as 1 dc, ch 1), work 1 dc in the same st, (V st made), 1 dc in each of the next 5 (7, 9, 9) sts (left sleeve), 1 V st in the next st, 1 dc in each of the 14 (16, 18, 18) sts (back),

1 V st in the next st, 1 dc in each of the next 5 (7, 9, 9) sts (right sleeve), 1 V st in the next st, 1 dc in each of the next 4 (6, 8, 8) sts (front), sl st in the V st to join—36 (44, 52, 52) sts.

Increase pattern begins – Continue increasing the yoke for the size you are working on.

Rnd 2: Ch 3, work 1 dc in ch-1 sp (V st made), 1 dc in each st across to the next V st (left sleeve), work 1 V st in ch-1 sp, 1 dc in each st across to the next V st (back), work 1 V st in ch-1 sp, 1 dc in each st across to the next V st (right sleeve), work 1 V st in ch-1 sp, 1 dc in each st across, ending with last st in the sl st join (front), sl st in the V st to join—44 (52, 60, 60) sts.

Rnds 3-4 (5, 7, 9):

Rep Round 2, increasing each section (sleeve, back, sleeve, front) by 2 sts each round. Ending with—60 (76, 100, 116) sts.

SEPARATE BODY AND SLEEVES

Body

Rnd 1: Skip over the left sleeve section to the next V st, sl st in the V, sl st in the next dc, ch 2, work 1 dc in the same st and in each st across to the next V, 22 (26, 32, 36) sts, sk V st and right sleeve section, 1 dc in 2nd dc of the next V st and in each st across, 12 (16, 22, 26) sts, rev sl st in the first dc to join—34 (42, 54, 62) sts.

Rnd 2: Ch 2, 1 dc in the first st and in each st around, rev sl st in the first dc to join—34 (42, 54, 62) sts.

Rounds 3-6 (7, 11, 13): Rep Round 2. Crochet to the desired length.

Band

The band is joined as you go to the body edge.

Row 1: Ch 5 (6, 6, 7), 1 sc in the 2nd ch from hook and in each ch across, sk first st at the body edge, sl st in the next 2 sts (body edge), turn—4 (5, 5, 6) sts.

Row 2: Sk sl sts, 1 sc in the blo of each st across, turn—4 (5, 5, 6) sts.

Row 3: Ch 1, work 1 sc in the blo of each st across, sl st in next 2 sts (body edge), turn—4 (5, 5, 6) sts.

Rows 4-34 (42, 54, 62): Rep Row 2 & 3 ending on Row 2. In the last Row, ch 1, with RS facing sl st band together, fasten off and weave in ends.

SLEEVES

Right Sleeve

Rnd 1: Put a slip knot on the hook; at the underarm, work a sl st in the first V st, sl st in the next V st, sl st in the next dc, ch 2, 1 dc in the same st, 1 dc in each st around, sl st in the first dc to join—13 (17, 23, 27) sts. Fasten off and weave in tails. Use tails to sew in any holes.

Left Sleeve

Rnd 1 (RS):

Put a slip knot on the hook at the underarm to the left, sl st in the first dc, ch 2, 1 dc in the same st, 1 dc in each st around, sl st in the first dc to join—13 (17, 23, 27) sts. Fasten off and weave in tails. Use tails to sew in any holes.

8. Alpine Crochet Sweater

Materials

- Yarn: Premier Cotton Fair (#2 weight)

  Color A: Turquoise

  Color B: Silver

- Hook

  Size H/5mm crochet hook

  Size I/5.5mm crochet hook

  Size J/6mm crochet hook

- Stitch markers (optional)
- Tapestry needle
- Tape measure

Finished Measurements

Neck - 10 inches

Chest - 15 inches

Belly - 17 inches

Length - 14 inches

Notes

- This pattern uses Honeycomb stitch and Alpine stitch. You will need to be familiar with these stitches to complete the project.
- FPDC in Alpine section is worked on the previous row of double crochets two rows below.
- This sweater is worked from top to bottom in both rounds and rows. Pay attention to the transition.
- Beginning ch 1 or ch 2 does not count as a stitch.

- At the end of each round, sl st in the first stitch from the round to join unless otherwise noted.
- The sizing provided in this pattern is approximate. Depending on your tension, the finished measurements may vary by about 1/2 inch.
- You may try using a different weight yarn and larger or smaller hook size to obtain your desired measurements.

Pattern

NECK/COLLAR SECTION

Ribbing [with 5mm hook and color A]

Row 1: Ch 27. Hdc in 3rd ch from hook and across. (25)

Row 2: Ch 2. Turn. Hdc blo in first st and across. (25)

Row 3 - 26: Repeat row 2. Ch 1 at the end.

Do not cut yarn. Fold piece in half, sl st to join the first 12 sts. (Figure 1)

Sl st in the remaining 13 sts on top side. (Figure 2)

Rotate piece clockwise.

Ch 1. Sc in corner st (same st as the last sl st), sc along side evenly. (40)

Rotate piece clockwise.

Ch 1. Sl st in corner st (same st as the last sc), sl st in next 12 sts on bottom side.

Cut yarn and tie off.

MAIN BODY SECTION

[with 6mm hook and color B]

Attach yarn to front center of collar where the neck piece was joined with sl st. (Figure 1 where stitch marker is)

Rnd 1: Ch 1. Sc 40 sts around evenly. (40)

Rnd 2: Ch1. Sc in same st, sc 3, inc, *sc 4, inc*, repeat *-* to end. (48)

Rnd 3: Ch 1. Sc in same st and around. (48)

Honeycomb stitch section

[switch to ROW]

Row 4: Ch 1. Turn. WS. Lsc below ch 1 st, sc, *lsc, sc*, repeat *-* to end. (48)

Sl st to top of first lsc to join.

Row 5: Ch 1. Turn. RS. Sc in same st, *fbsc, sc*, repeat *-* to end, fbsc in last st. (48)

Sl st to top of first sc to join.

Row 6: Ch 1. Turn. WS. Sc in same st, *lsc, sc*, repeat *-* to end, lsc in last st. (48)

Sl st to top of first sc to join.

Row 7: Ch 1. Turn. RS. Fbsc around the last bar and first bar from previous row, sc, *fbsc, sc*, repeat *-* to end. (48)

Sl st to top of first fbsc to join.

Do not turn.

86

[continue in ROUNDS]

Round 8: Ch 1. Sc in same st, sc, inc, *sc 5, inc*, repeat *-* until last 3 sts, sc in last 3 sts. (56)

ARMHOLES

Round 9: Ch 1. Sc in same st, sc 4, ch 12, skip next 10 sts, sc 28, ch 12, skip next 10 sts, sc in last 3 sts. (36 sts, 24 chs)

Round 10: Ch 1. Sc in same st and around. (60)

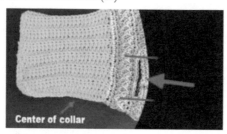

Center of collar

[switch to ROW]

Row 11: Ch 1. Turn. WS. Lsc below ch 1 st, sc, lsc, sc, sc2tog, sc 8, sc2tog, *lsc, sc* 14 times, sc2tog, sc 8, sc2tog, *lsc, sc* twice. (56)

Sl st to top of first lsc to join.

Note: For Row 11 only, make lsc 3 rows down instead of 2 rows down.

Row 12: Ch 1. Turn. RS. Sc in same st, *fbsc, sc* twice, fbsc around 1 bar, sc 9, fbsc around 1 bar, sc, *fbsc, sc* 13 times, fbsc around 1 bar, sc 9, fbsc around 1 bar, sc, fbsc. (56)

Sl st to top of first sc to join.

Row 13: Ch 1. Turn. WS. Sc in same st, *lsc, sc*, repeat *-* to end. Lsc in the last st. (56)

Sl st to top of first sc to join.

Row 14: Ch 1. Turn. RS. Fbsc around the last bar and first bar from previous row, *sc, fbsc*, repeat *-* to end. Sc in the last st. (56)

Sl st to top of first fbsc to join.

Row 15: Ch 1. Turn. WS. Lsc below ch 1 st, *sc, lsc*, repeat *-* to end. Sc in the last st. (56)

Sl st to top of first lsc to join.

Row 16: Ch 1. Turn. RS. Sc in same st, *fbsc, sc*, repeat *-* to end. Fbsc in the last st. (56)

Sl st to top of first sc to join.

Row 17: Ch 1. Turn. WS. Sc in same st, *lsc, sc*, repeat *-* to end. Lsc in the last st. (56)

Sl st to top of first sc to join.

Row 18: Ch 1. Turn. RS. Fbsc around the last bar and first bar from previous row, *sc, fbsc*, repeat *-* to end. Sc in the last st. (56)

Sl st to top of first sc to join.

End Honeycomb stitch section

Do not turn. Working on RS. [continue in ROUNDS & switch to color A]

Note: For Round 19, crochet loosely so the round is not too tight

Round 19: Ch 1. Sc in same st, sc in back bump in next st and around. (56)

[switch to 5.5mm hook]

Round 20: ch 1. Hdc in same st and around. (56)

Alpine stitch section

Round 21: Ch 2. Dc in same st, fpdc, *dc, fpdc*, repeat *-* to end. (56)

Round 22: Ch 1. Sc in same st and around. (56)

Round 23: Ch 2. Fpdc in same st, dc, *fpdc, dc*, repeat *-* to end. (56)

Round 24: Ch 1. Sc in same st and around. (56)

Round 25-28: Repeat rounds 21-24.

Round 29: Ch 2. Dc in same st, fpdc, *dc, fpdc* 5 times, inc, *fpdc, dc* 14 times, fpdc, inc, *fpdc, dc*, repeat *-* until last st, fpdc in last st. (58)

Round 30: Ch 1. Sc in same st and around. (58)

Round 31: Ch 2. Fpdc in same st, dc, *fpdc, dc*, repeat *-* to end following the Alpine Stitch pattern. (60)

Note: In Round 31, when you get to the inc sts in Round 29,

(1) fpdc around the first dc (Figure 4),

(2) dc in next st at top of second dc (Figure 4),

(3) fpdc around the second dc (Figure 5),

(4) dc in next st (Figure 5).

Then continue with the normal Alpine Stitch pattern

Figure 4   **Figure 5**

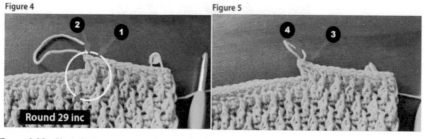

Round 32: Ch 1. Sc in same st and around. (60)

Round 33: Ch 2. Dc in same st, fpdc, *dc, fpdc*, repeat *-* to end. (60)

Round 34: Ch 1. Sc in same st and around. (60)

Round 35: Ch 2. Fpdc in same st, dc, *fpdc, dc*, repeat *-* to end. (60)

Round 36: Ch 1. Sc in same st and around. (60)

Join round. Cut yarn and tie off.

Flatten the piece by the center of the collar. Find the center on belly side in the last round. (Figure 7)

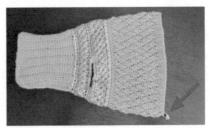

Place stitch markers in the two center stitches. (Figure 8)

Place a stitch marker in the 8th st from center sts on each side. These will be the first and the last st of your rows from here on. (Figure 9)

Attach yarn to first st. RS.

[switch to ROW]

Row 37: Ch 1. Sc in same st, hdc, *fpdc, dc*, repeat *-* until the last 2 sts, hdc in next st, sc in last st. (44)

Row 38: Ch 1. Turn. WS. Sc in same st and across. (44)

Row 39: Ch 1. Turn. RS. Sc in same st, hdc, *dc, fpdc*, repeat *-* until the last 2 sts, hdc in next st, sc in last st. (44)

Row 40: Ch 1. Turn. WS. Sc in same st and across. (44)

Row 41: Ch 1. Turn. RS. Sc in same st, hdc, *fpdc, dc*, repeat *-* until the last 2 sts, hdc in next st, sc in last st. (44)

Row 42: Ch 1. Turn. WS. Sc in same st and across. (44)

Row 43: Ch 1. Turn. RS. Sc in same st, hdc, *dc, fpdc*, repeat *-* until the last 2 sts, hdc in next st, sc in last st. (44)

End Alpine stitch section

Do not turn. Do not cut yarn.

Continue on to Ribbing section.

RIBBING SECTION

Rotate piece clockwise. Base round:

(1) Work along the short edge to crochet 6 sts* evenly,

(2) sc2tog in the "last st "from Row 36 and the st after,

(3) sc in next 14,

(4) sc2tog in next st and the "first st" from Row 36,

(5) sc 6 sts* evenly along the other short edge,

(6) sc in next 44. (72)

Continue on to start ribbing.

Start ribbing: Ch 8

Row 1: Hdc 3rd ch from hook and across. (6)

Row 2: Sl st in next 3 sts. Turn. Hdc blo until last st, hdc in both Loops in last st. (6)

Row 3: Ch 1. Turn. Hdc blo to end toward base round. (6)

Repeat row 2 and Row 3 around the base round until the last 3 sts.

Sl st in last 3 sts.

Sl st to join first row and last row of ribbing together.

Cut yarn and tie off.

FINISHING UP

Tidy up armholes Attach yarn in any st. in the armhole. Ch 1. Sc in same st and across evenly. (26). Sew in all ends.

Made in United States
Troutdale, OR
12/04/2024

25778598R00053